WONDER *of* WONDERS

Statue of Bonhoeffer on west facade of Westminster Abbey

WONDER *of* WONDERS

CHRISTMAS *with* DIETRICH BONHOEFFER

Dietrich Bonhoeffer

Translated from the German by O. C. Dean Jr.

WESTMINSTER
JOHN KNOX PRESS
LOUISVILLE · KENTUCKY

© 2015 Westminster John Knox Press

First edition
Published by Westminster John Knox Press
Louisville, Kentucky

Translated by O. C. Dean Jr. from *Wunder aller Wunder* published in 2013 by Güterslother Verlagshaus, Gütersloh, Germany, in der Verlagsgruppe Random House GmbH, München

Selections originally published in Dietrich Bonhoeffer Werke (DBW)
© Gütersloher Verlagshaus, Gütersloh, in der Verlagsgruppe Random House GmbH, München.

9: DBW 10/469	24: DBW 8/471	36: DBW 10/437	50: DBW 8, 19
10: DBW 10/484	27: DBW 8/197	39: DBW 10, 481f.	53: DBW 8,36
13: DBW 10/544	28: DBW 8/207	41: DBW 15, 491	54: DBW 10, 585
14, 17: DBW 10/479f.	32: DBW 10, 586f.	42, 44: DBW 16, 636f.	
21, 23: DBW 10/529	35: DBW 16/634	48: DBW 15, 498	

15 16 17 18 19 20 21 22 23 24—10 9 8 7 6 5 4 3 2 1

Scripture quotations, unless otherwise indicated, are from the New Revised Standard Version of the Bible, copyright © 1989 by the Division of Christian Education of the National Council of the Churches of Christ in the U.S.A., and are used by permission.

Interior photos: © Renata Sedmakova/Shutterstock.com; © TTstudio/Dollar Photo Club; © Burben/Shutterstock.com; © iStock.com/Vintervit; © robert cicchetti/Dollar Photo Club; © iStock.com/dennisvdw; © Kochergin/Dollar Photo Club; © Lilyana Vynogradova/Shutterstock.com; © Deymos.HR/Dollar Photo Club; © Lars Johansson/Dollar Photo Club; © Nikolai Sorokin/Dollar Photo Club; © pwollinga/Dollar Photo Club; © pierluigipalazzi/Dollar Photo Club; © jefunne/Dollar Photo Club; © Pauline/Dollar Photo Club; © iStock.com/SafakOguz; © lily/Dollar Photo Club; © Delphotostock/Dollar Photo Club; © vinbergv/Dollar Photo Club; © iStock.com/coloroftime; © knowlesgallery/Dollar Photo Club; © Farmer/Dollar Photo Club; © Gucio_55/Dollar Photo Club; © Mikhail Markovskiy/Dollar Photo Club; © Delmas Lehman/Dollar Photo Club; © Grisha Bruev/Shutterstock.com

Book design by Allison Taylor
Cover design by Barbara LeVan Fisher / levanfisherstudio.com

Library of Congress Cataloging-in-Publication Data

Bonhoeffer, Dietrich, 1906-1945.
  [Works. Selections. English.]
  Wonder of wonders : Christmas with Dietrich Bonhoeffer / Dietrich Bonhoeffer ; translated from the German by O. C. Dean Jr.
    pages cm
  ISBN 978-0-664-26045-3 (alk. paper)
1. Theology. 2. Advent. 3. Christmas. 4. Bonhoeffer, Dietrich, 1906-1945. I. Title.
  BX4827.B57A25 2015
  242--dc23
                                                                                                2014049527

Printed in the United States of America

Most Westminster John Knox Press books are available at special quantity discounts
when purchased in bulk by corporations, organizations, and special-interest groups.
For more information, please e-mail SpecialSales@wjkbooks.com.

CONTENTS

IN SEARCH *of the* SOUL

In our time there is a seeking,

an anxious groping and searching for divine things.

A great loneliness has come over our time,

a loneliness that is found only where godforsakenness reigns.

In the midst of our large cities,

in the greatest, most frantic activity of untold masses of people,

we see the greatest amount of loneliness and homelessness.

But the longing grows that the time will nonetheless come again

when God dwells among people,

when God lets himself be found.

In the middle of this frantic activity

and vociferous extolling of new ways and means

stands the one word of Jesus Christ:

"I am with you . . ." (Matt. 28:20).

He does not prescribe ways in which we can reach him.

Rather, he says quite simply:

"I am with you."

11

None of us lives a life so rushed that it is impossible for us

to find even ten minutes a day, in the morning or evening,

when we can let everything around us become quiet

and submit ourselves completely to eternity,

when we can let it speak to us and ask it about ourselves.

In that way we can look very deeply within ourselves

and quite far beyond ourselves.

That might happen by looking at a few Bible verses or, even better,

by becoming utterly free and letting our soul make its way

to the Father's house, to its home,

in which it will find rest.

Listen! I am standing at the door, knocking;

if you hear my voice and open the door,

I will come in to you and eat with you,

and you with me.

Revelation 3:20

Every day create for yourself

a few minutes of solitude

and reflect on the coming day

or the day before

and on the people you encountered.

Think about yourself and what you lack,

but never just root around within yourself.

Rather, share those solitary hours with

the One who also knows your secrets.

✳   ✳   ✳

For God alone my soul waits in silence,

for my hope is from him.

He alone is my rock and my salvation,

my fortress; I shall not be shaken.

On God rests my deliverance and my honor;

my mighty rock, my refuge is in God.

Psalm 62:5–7

15

Like a song from old times,

like a medieval image painted on gold leaf,

like the memory of childhood days,

the sound of the wonderful word of the soul

has grown foreign to us.

If there is still in our day—in the age of machines,

of economic battles, of the reign of fashion

and sports—something like the soul,

then it's not just a dear childhood memory

like so many others.

The little word "soul" sounds just so wonderful and strange

in the confusion and shouting of voices that extol it;

the language is so soft and still

that we hardly hear it anymore over the raging

and roaring going on within us.

But the word speaks a language

that is full of the greatest responsibility and deepest seriousness.

Hey, you! Human being!

You have a soul!

See that you don't lose it,

that you don't wake up one day from the frenzy of life—

professional and private life—

and see that you have become hollow inside,

a plaything of events,

a leaf driven back and forth

and blown away by the wind:

that you are without a soul.

It is the life that God has given us;

it is what God has loved about us,

what he—from his eternity—has touched.

It is love in us and longing and holy restlessness

and responsibility and happiness and pain;

it is divine breath breathed into mortal being.

ADVENT: WAITING *is an* ART

Celebrating Advent means being able to wait.

Waiting is an art that our impatient age has forgotten.

Those who do not know how it feels to anxiously struggle

with the deepest questions of life, of their life,

and to patiently look forward with anticipation

until the truth is revealed,

cannot even dream of the splendor of the moment

in which clarity is illuminated for them.

And for those who do not want to win the friendship

and love of another person—

who do not expectantly open up their soul

to the soul of the other person,

until friendship and love come,

until they make their entrance—

for such people the deepest blessing of the one life

of two intertwined souls will remain forever hidden.

Whoever does not know

the austere blessedness of waiting—

that is, of hopefully doing without—

will never experience

the full blessing of fulfillment.

For the greatest,

most profound,

tenderest things in the world,

we must wait.

It happens here not in a storm

but according to the divine laws

of sprouting, growing,

and becoming.

Night, put out whatever is burning;

grant me total forgetfulness;

be charitable to me.

Night, do your gentle work;

in you I put my trust.

But the night is wise and mighty,

wiser than I and mightier than the day.

What no earthly power can do—

where thoughts and feelings,

defiance and tears must fail—

that is what night pours over me

in rich abundance.

We are silent in the early hours of each day,

because God is supposed to have the first word,

and we are silent before going to sleep,

because to God also belongs the last word.

We are silent solely for the sake of the word,

not in order to show dishonor to the word

but in order to honor and receive it properly.

Silence ultimately means nothing

but waiting for God's word

and coming away blessed by God's word.

✳ ✳ ✳

Life in a prison cell may well be compared to Advent:

one waits, hopes, and does this, that, or the other—

things that are really of no consequence—

the door is shut, and can only be opened *from the outside.*

Letter from Bonhoeffer at Tegel prison
to Eberhard Bethge, November 21, 1943[1]

1. Dietrich Bonhoeffer, *Letters and Papers from Prison: New Greatly Enlarged Edition*, ed. Eberhard Bethge (New York: Touchstone, 1997), 135.

EVENING PRAYER

My Lord God, I thank you

that you have brought this day to an end;

I thank you that you let body and soul come to rest.

Your hand was over me;

it protected me and preserved me.

Forgive all the faintheartedness, lack of faith,

and unrighteousness of this day,

and help me to gladly forgive those who have wronged me.

Let me sleep in peace under your protection,

and preserve me from the assaults of darkness.

I commend to you those close to me;

I commend to you this house;

I commend to you my body and my soul.

O God, may your holy name be praised.

Amen.

CHRISTMAS: MIRACLE
of MIRACLES

We all come with different personal feelings to the Christmas festival.

One comes with pure joy as he looks forward

to this day of rejoicing, of friendships renewed, and of love. . . .

Others look for a moment of peace under the Christmas tree,

peace from the pressures of daily work. . . .

Others again approach Christmas with great apprehension.

It will be no festival of joy to them.

Personal sorrow is painful especially on this day

for those whose loneliness is deepened at Christmastime. . . .

And despite it all, Christmas comes.

Whether we wish it or not, whether we are sure or not,

we must hear the words once again: Christ the Savior is here!

The world that Christ comes to save

is our fallen and lost world. None other.

Sermon to a German-speaking church
in Havana, Cuba, December 21, 1930[1]

1. Dietrich Bonhoeffer, *Dietrich Bonhoeffer's Christmas Sermons*, ed. and trans. Edwin Robertson (Grand Rapids: Zondervan, 2005), 151. By Christmas of 1940, the Nazis had forbidden Bonhoeffer to preach publicly. This excerpt comes from a Christmas sermon he wrote that was circulated in print.

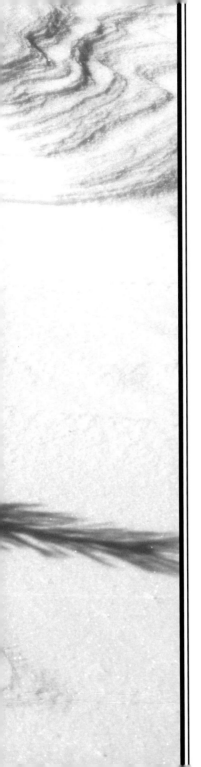

The topic here is the birth of a child—

not the revolutionary deed of a strong man,

not the bold discovery of a wise person,

not the godly work of a saint.

It really goes beyond all comprehension:

the birth of a child is supposed to lead

to the great turning point of all things and

to bring the salvation and redemption of all humanity.

What kings and leaders of nations, philosophers and artists,

founders of religions and teachers of morals

have tried in vain to do—

that now happens through a newborn child.

That is the mystery of the redemption of the world;

everything past and everything future is encompassed here.

The infinite mercy of the almighty God comes to us,

descends to us in the form of a child, his Son.

Having peace means knowing oneself borne,

knowing oneself loved, knowing oneself protected;

it means being able to be still, quite still.

Having peace with people means

being able to build unshakably on their faithfulness;

it means knowing oneself at one with them,

knowing oneself forgiven by them.

Having peace means having a homeland in the unrest of the world;

it means having solid ground under one's feet.

Though the waves may now rage and break,

they can no longer rob me of my peace.

My peace has made me free from the world,

made me strong against the world,

made me ready for the other world.

But the fact that we are to have such peace with God

is something that goes beyond all human comprehension,

beyond all reason.

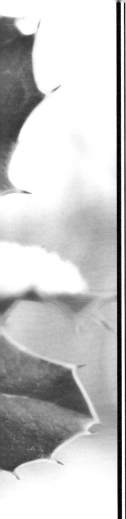

My soul is silent before God.

Being silent really means

no longer being able to say anything;

it means feeling as if a strange,

loving hand is laid on our lips

and tells us to be silent.

Being silent means

being blessed in the sight

of the One longed for and loved;

it means devoting oneself completely;

it means capitulating to the greater power

of the Other, the totally Other;

it means for a moment no longer seeing oneself at all,

but seeing only the Other.

Yet it also means waiting,

waiting to see if the Other has something to say to us.

For a child has been born for us,

a son given to us;

authority rests upon his shoulders;

and he is named

Wonderful Counselor,

Mighty God,

Everlasting Father,

Prince of Peace.

His authority shall grow continually,

and there shall be endless peace.

Isaiah 9:6–7

"Wonderful Counselor" (Isa. 9:6) is the name of this child.

In him the wonder of all wonders has taken place;

the birth of the Savior-child has gone forth from God's eternal counsel.

In the form of a human child, God gave us his Son;

God became human, the Word became flesh (John 1:14).

That is the wonder of the love of God for us,

and it is God's unfathomable wise counsel that this love wins us and saves us.

"Mighty God" (Isa. 9:6) is the name of this child.

The child in the manger is none other than God himself.

Nothing greater can be said: God became a child.

In the Jesus child of Mary lives the almighty God.

Wait a minute! Don't speak; stop thinking! Stand still before this statement!

"Everlasting Father" (Isa. 9:6)—how can this be the name of the child?

Only because in this child the everlasting fatherly love of God is revealed,

and the child wants nothing other than to bring to earth the love of the Father.

So the Son is one with the Father, and whoever sees the Son sees the Father.

"Prince of Peace" (Isa. 9:6)—where God comes in love to human beings

and unites with them, there peace is made

between God and humankind and among people.

Are you afraid of God's wrath?

Then go to the child in the manger and receive there the peace of God.

Have you fallen into strife and hatred with your sister or brother?

Come and see how God, out of pure love,

has become our brother and wants to reconcile us with each other.

In the world, power reigns.

This child is the Prince of Peace. Where he is, peace reigns.

"Wonderful Counselor, Mighty God,

Everlasting Father, Prince of Peace"—

thus do we speak of the cradle of Bethlehem;

thus do our words pour forth when we regard the divine child;

thus do we attempt to define with concepts

what is summed up for us in the one name: Jesus.

THE POWER *of* HOPE

We are going into a new year.

Many human plans and mistakes,

much hostility and need

will determine our path.

But as long as we stay with Jesus

and go with him,

we can be certain that we too

can encounter nothing that God

has not already foreseen, willed, and promised.

Are not five sparrows sold for two pennies?

Yet not one of them is forgotten in God's sight.

But even the hairs of your head are all counted.

Do not be afraid; you are of more value than many sparrows.

—Luke 12:6–7

Since time is the most precious thing

we have at our disposal—

because it is the hardest thing to reclaim—

whenever we look back,

we are disturbed by the thought

of the possibility of lost time.

Lost would be the time

in which we have not lived as human beings

or had human experiences—

not learned, not created,

not enjoyed, not suffered.

Lost time is unfulfilled, empty time.

That certainly does not describe these past years.

We have lost much—

immeasurably much—

but the time was not lost.

By nature, optimism is not a view of the present situation

but a living power, the power of hope where others are resigned,

the power to hold one's head high

when everything seems to be going wrong,

the power to bear setbacks,

the power never leaves the future to the adversary

but lays claim to it for oneself.

Certainly, there is also a dumb, cowardly optimism

that must be scorned.

But optimism as the will to the future

should not be disparaged by anyone,

even if it is wrong a hundred times.

It is the health of life, which the sick are not supposed to infect.

⁂ ⁂ ⁂

May the God of hope fill you with all joy and peace in believing,

so that you may abound in hope by the power of the Holy Spirit.

—*Romans 15:13*

Great things are promised,

and they are imminent.

Incredible events are proclaimed,

events that no human ear has heard;

unrevealed mysteries are opened up.

The earth and humankind

are already quaking under their advance.

And a prophetic voice cries into a frightened world:

The kingdom of heaven has come near.

The Lord God himself is coming,

the Creator and Judge.

He comes with love for humankind.

He wants to take humanity home

to the everlasting banquet.

He is coming.

Are you ready?

A Short Biography of Dietrich Bonhoeffer

February 4, 1906	Born in Breslau, Germany (now Wroclaw, Poland)
1923–27	Study of Evangelical Theology in Tübingen, Rome, and Berlin, followed by a doctoral degree and qualification for university lecturing (1930)
1928–29	Vicar in Barcelona
1930–31	Year of study at Union Theological Seminary, New York
1931	Privatdozent and university pastor in Berlin; ecumenical work
1933	Beginning of ecclesiastical resistance work; pastor in London
1935	Leadership of an illegal seminary for preachers in Finkenwalde
1937	Closing of the seminary by police; continued illegal work
1939	Trip to New York in summer; return to Berlin before start of war
1940	Beginning of service as an informer for the Resistance; started working on his book *Ethik* (*Ethics*)
1941–42	Conspiratorial trips to Switzerland, Norway, Sweden, and Italy
1943	Engagement to Maria von Wedemeyer in January
April 5, 1943	Arrest and incarceration in the Berlin-Tegel prison; lively correspondence with Eberhard Bethge; foundations for his work *Widerstand und Ergebung* (*Letters and Papers from Prison*)
October 8, 1944	Transfer to the main prison of the Gestapo
February 7, 1945	Deportation to the concentration camp Buchenwald
April 5, 1945	Condemnation to death by Adolf Hitler
April 8, 1945	Transfer to the concentration camp Flossenbürg
April 9, 1945	Death sentence carried out